Good Question!

What Makes a Tornado Twist?
AND OTHER QUESTIONS ABOUT . . .
Weather

STERLING CHILDREN'S BOOKS
New York

STERLING CHILDREN'S BOOKS
New York

An Imprint of Sterling Publishing
387 Park Avenue South
New York, NY 10016

Photo Credits: 14: © eyecrave/iStockphoto; 19: © Australian Land, City, People Scape Photographer/Getty Images; 22: Image Science and Analysis Laboratory/Johnson Space Center/NASA; 30: © Ryan McGinnis/Getty Images

ISBN 978-1-4549-0682-7 [hardcover]
ISBN 978-1-4549-0683-4 [paperback]

Library of Congress Cataloging-in-Publication Data

Carson, Mary Kay.

What makes a tornado twist? : and other questions about weather / Mary Kay Carson ; [illustrated by] Louis Mackay.
    pages cm. -- [Good question!]
    ISBN 978-1-4549-0683-4 (pbk.) -- ISBN 978-1-4549-0682-7 (hardcover) 1. Weather--Juvenile literature. I. Mackay, Louis, illustrator. II. Title.
    QC981.3.C3724 2014
    551.6--dc23
                                2013042129
Distributed in Canada by Sterling Publishing
c/o Canadian Manda Group, 165 Dufferin Street
Toronto, Ontario, Canada M6K 3H6
Distributed in the United Kingdom by GMC Distribution Services
Castle Place, 166 High Street, Lewes, East Sussex, England BN7 1XU
Distributed in Australia by Capricorn Link (Australia) Pty. Ltd.
P.O. Box 704, Windsor, NSW 2756, Australia

Design by Andrea Miller
Paintings by Louis Mackay

For information about custom editions, special sales, and premium and corporate purchases,
please contact Sterling Special Sales at 800-805-5489 or specialsales@sterlingpublishing.com.

Manufactured in China
Lot #:
2 4 6 8 10 9 7 5 3 1
04/14

www.sterlingpublishing.com/kids

CONTENTS

How's the weather?

Take a peek outside. Is it sunny and warm, or cloudy and cold? Is this a windy and wet week, or is it a calm and dry morning? The weather changes from minute to minute and place to place. Weather constantly changes because so does the air around and above us. Weather describes the air in one place at a particular time. The weather now isn't going to be the same as the weather later. And the weather here isn't the same as the weather somewhere else!

Weather describes all kinds of things about the air. How cold or hot and damp or dry it is. How fast or slow the air is moving is weather, too. So is what the air carries, like clouds, snow, rain, or storms.

What are the three ingredients of weather?

Weather comes in many types. How many can you think of? No matter the storm, wind, or cloud you're imagining, all are made with the same three ingredients. Air, water, and sun create all the world's weather. The sun's heat, the air, and Earth's water all affect one another. They heat and cool, moisten and dry, and churn and mix. Together they create all weather, from snowstorms to sunny afternoons.

LOOK UP AND LOOK AROUND! YOU'LL SEE EVERYTHING NEEDED TO MAKE WEATHER ALL AROUND YOU—AIR, SUNLIGHT, AND WATER!

Why is the Amazon hotter than the North Pole?

The sun powers all weather. Its energy bathes our planet in light and heat, but not evenly. Sunlight soaks the warm belt around Earth's middle, the equator. Meanwhile, the top and bottom of Earth, its poles, are always cold. Why? The sunlight that hits the equator is direct and strong, like a flashlight's bright beam. The poles receive less direct sunlight. The heat and light of this weaker sunlight is more spread out, so it is less concentrated.

Temperature is how hot or cold something is. The air outside your school has a temperature, and so does the ocean near Florida. Where a place is on the globe affects its temperature. So does the type of land or water covering that place. The water in oceans and lakes warms up more slowly than land. This is why the sunny swimming pool can still be cold from the night before, even on a hot day. Color makes a difference, too. Like black car seats in summer, dark rocks and soil soak up more heat than white snowfields and sand.

What causes the seasons?

Is it warmer where you live in June or January? Temperatures change throughout the year in most places. The tilt of Earth creates the seasons. Earth both spins around like a top and moves around the sun. We complete one circle, or orbit, around the sun each year. Our planet turns around on a tilt, leaning to one side. This means that for part of Earth's yearly path around the sun, the top half leans toward the sun. The half leaning toward the sun gets more sunlight, is warmer, and has summer. Meanwhile the bottom half of Earth gets less sunlight, is colder, and has winter. Six months later, we're on the other side of the sun and Earth's tilt is opposite.

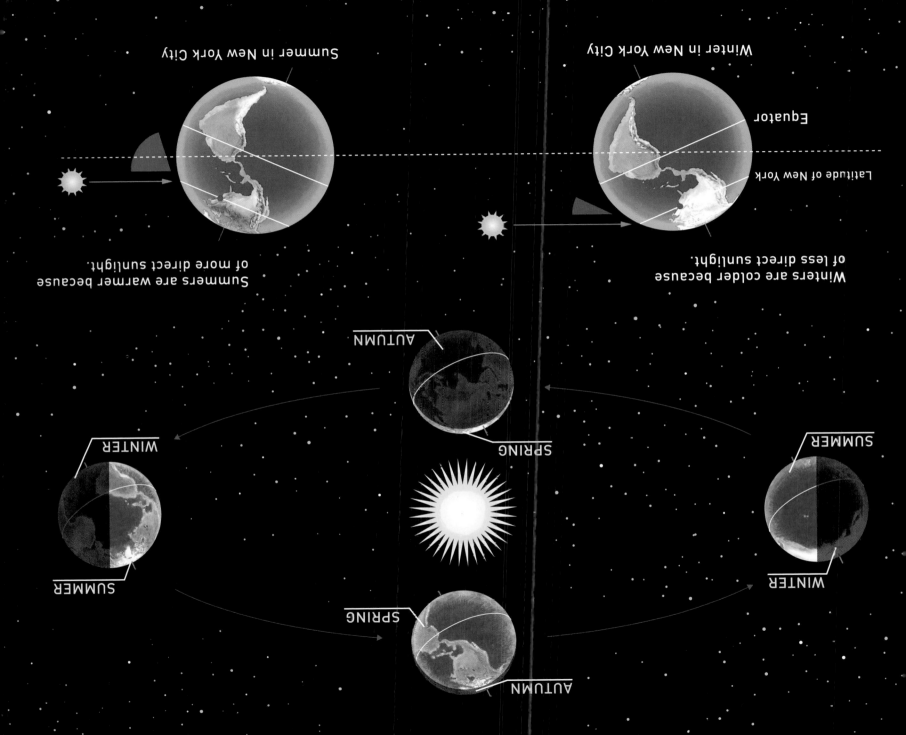

Summer in New York City

Summers are warmer because
of more direct sunlight.

Winter in New York City

Equator

Latitude of New York

Winters are colder because
of less direct sunlight.

AUTUMN

SPRING

WINTER

SUMMER

SUMMER

WINTER

SPRING

AUTUMN

Why does weather start in the sky?

Air is where weather happens. Air is all around us—and above us. Wrapped around Earth is a blanket of air called the atmosphere. The atmosphere is 300 miles or 483 kilometers (km) thick. That's about the width of Pennsylvania. Where the atmosphere ends, outer space begins. Most weather happens in the bottom 10 miles (16 km) or so of the atmosphere that stretches up from the land and oceans.

The air in our atmosphere is made up of invisible gases. Air is mostly oxygen—the gas you breathe—and nitrogen gas. When the sun lights up air, it scatters blue light that colors the sky. You can't see the gases in air, but air takes up space and has weight. Think of how air fills up a bike tire or balloon. Or how moving air—wind—can topple towers and push people over. Air is powerful stuff!

All the air in the atmosphere above Earth is very heavy. Like sleeping under a stack of covers, it pushes down and creates pressure. This pushing down force is called atmospheric pressure, or air pressure. It's a big player in weather because air pressure changes with temperature. Warm air weighs less and is lighter, so it rises up. A hot air balloon floats because its warmed, lighter air has less pressure. Cold air is heavier and has more pressure, and so it sinks. The differences in temperature create differences in air pressure that churn wind, form clouds, and sprout storms.

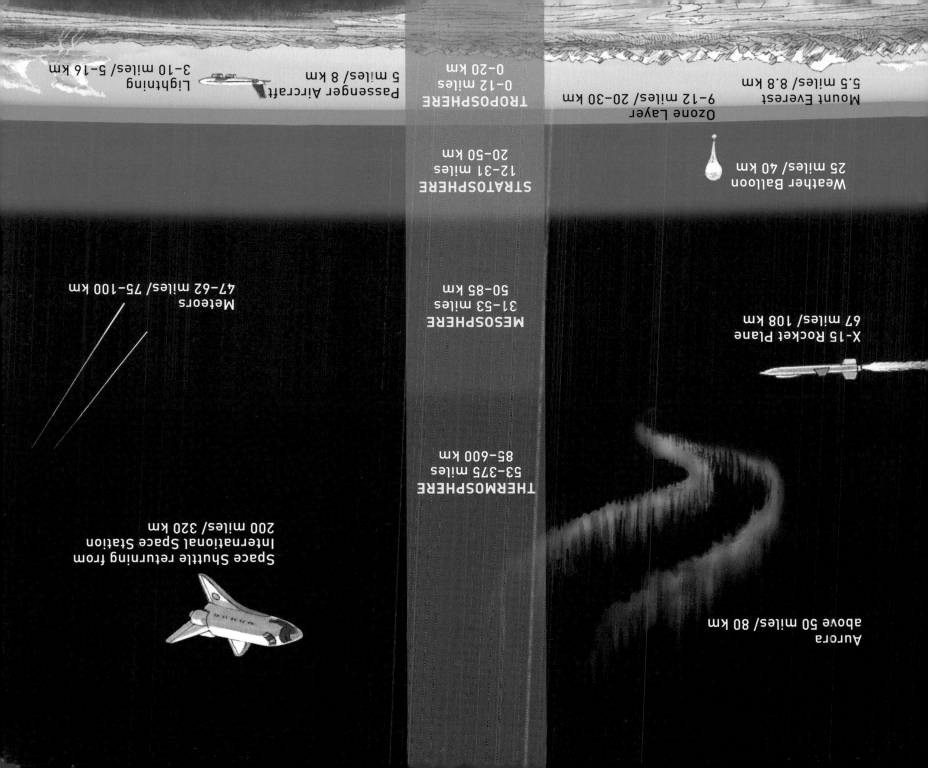

Lightning
3-10 miles/ 5-16 Km

Passenger Aircraft
5 miles/ 8 km

TROPOSPHERE
0-12 miles
0-20 Km

Ozone Layer
9-12 miles/ 20-30 km

Mount Everest
5.5 miles/ 8.8 km

STRATOSPHERE
12-31 miles
20-50 km

Weather Balloon
25 miles/ 40 Km

Meteors
47-62 miles/ 75-100 km

MESOSPHERE
31-53 miles
50-85 km

X-15 Rocket Plane
67 miles/ 108 km

THERMOSPHERE
53-375 miles
85-600 km

Space Shuttle returning from
International Space Station
200 miles/ 320 Km

Aurora
above 50 miles/ 80 km

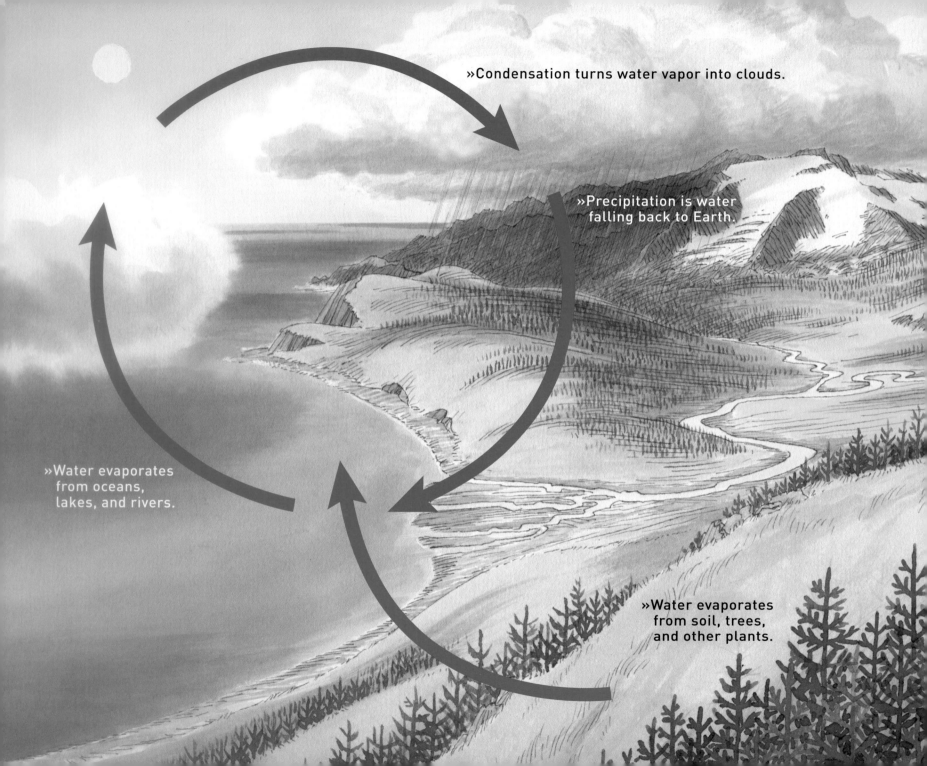

»Condensation turns water vapor into clouds.

»Precipitation is water falling back to Earth.

»Water evaporates from oceans, lakes, and rivers.

»Water evaporates from soil, trees, and other plants.

Why does it rain?

Water is amazing stuff. It does something no other substance can do. It goes back and forth between being a solid, a liquid, and a gas in natural conditions. Icicles melt, lakes freeze, and ponds dry up. Water's ability to easily switch from ice to liquid to gas creates weather. It makes moving water between Earth's atmosphere and surface possible. This is called the water cycle. It dries up ponds, melts snowmen, delivers rain, and freezes icebergs.

The sun's heat powers the water cycle. What happens to water in puddles, seas, rivers, soil, and plants when the sun heats them up? The water evaporates, changing from liquid to water vapor, which is a gas. When water vapor cools, it condenses, changing back to liquid. This is why cool nights leave dewdrops on lawns and bathroom mirrors fog up. Clouds form when cooling water vapor condenses into tiny floating drops of liquid. When those liquid drops grow too heavy, they fall back to Earth as precipitation—rain and snow. Rain refills ponds, streams, and seas that continue the water cycle when the sun shines.

What makes a rainbow?

Rain showers sometimes end with a lovely surprise. A beautiful arch of color across the sky—a rainbow! Raindrops create rainbows. The droplets act like tiny prisms, splitting sunlight into all its colors. A rainbow is really a full circle, not an arch. You can't see the bottom half of the circle because it disappears below the horizon. Rainbows show up after downpours when it's still raining nearby. In order to see a rainbow, the sun must be at your back while you look toward a rainy sky.

Why do clouds float?

Clouds are big floating heaps of water droplets. Condensation is the key to making clouds. Condensation happens when rising and cooling water vapor changes into water droplets. These tiny water droplets clump and collect together as a cloud. One cloud can hold thousands of gallons of water. How does something so heavy stay up in the air? A helium-filled balloon floats because helium is lighter than the gases in air. A cloud floats for the same reason. The moist, or humid, air in clouds is less dense than the dry air around them. Clouds float because they are lighter than air.

Clouds come in many shapes and range from white to dark gray. Clouds are made by weather and make weather. Clouds clue us in on what's going on in the air above us. The names of many clouds describe their shapes and their heights in the sky. Stratus clouds are layered and flat. Cumulus clouds are fluffy piled-up lumps. Cirrus clouds are thin and wispy. Clouds high up in the sky often begin with cirro-, like cirrostratus. Below them are clouds that start with alto-, like altocumulus. A cloud name with nimbo means it's making rain or snow, like cumulonimbus. Fog is a cloud very near the ground.

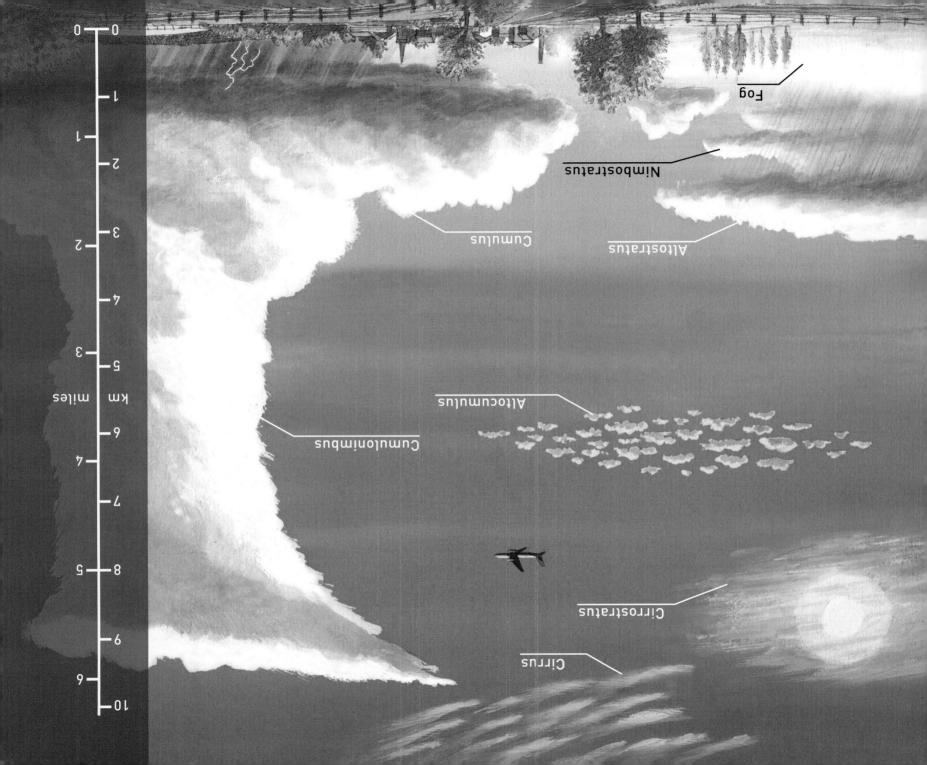

Is each snowflake unique?

It's true! Snowflakes are water frozen into crystal shapes with six sides. Tiny single snow crystals look similar. But those that grow into snowflakes become very complex. So many combinations of crystal patterns are possible that each snowflake that's ever fallen is unlikely to ever appear again. Snow is just one of the forms of water falling from clouds, called precipitation. Whether cloud droplets become snow or rain, hail or drizzle depends on weather! The temperature of the air all the way down to the ground makes a difference. So does the kind of cloud it falls from.

It takes a good ruler to tell the difference between rain and drizzle. Drizzle becomes rain once the water drops are bigger than 0.02 inches (0.5 millimeters) across. When raindrops freeze as they fall, they become sleet. If raindrops freeze as they hit the ground, they're called freezing rain. That's the slippery stuff that gives branches and sidewalks an icy coating. Snow is made of ice crystals that fall from clouds and don't melt on their way down. Hail is born inside a thunderstorm cloud as balls of ice. Each hailstone adds on layers of ice as winds toss it up into cloud's coldest parts over and over, until it falls to the ground. What's your favorite precipitation?

What causes stormy weather?

Storms are violent weather changes. A storm is a major change, or disturbance, in the atmosphere that creates wind, clouds, rain, snow, and other dicey weather. The atmospheric upset comes from battling air masses. An air mass is a huge body, or area, of air with the same temperature and humidity. An air mass gets its temperature and humidity where it formed. An air mass created over the tropical ocean is warm and humid, while one made over Antarctica is cold and dry. Once made, an air mass goes on the move. When different air masses meet, they don't easily mix. They crash into each other, pushing and shoving. The border where the two meet and battle is called a front.

Fronts are where air masses wage war. A front gets its name from the winning air mass, the one that's moving forward. A warm front has a warm air mass sliding up and over the heavier air of a cold air mass. Warmer, moist air behind the warm front pushes it forward over the cold air mass it's replacing. But in a cold front, a cold air mass is the advancing invader. It sneaks under and shoves up the lighter warm air. Cooler, dry air behind the cold front drives it forward.

Which way the wind blows makes a difference on the weather battlefield. Whichever air mass, warm or cold, has the stronger winds behind it advances and is the winner. With either kind of front, warm air ends up rising, which creates rain or snow clouds. When neither air mass is winning, a stationary front forms. It's a weather standoff that can last for days.

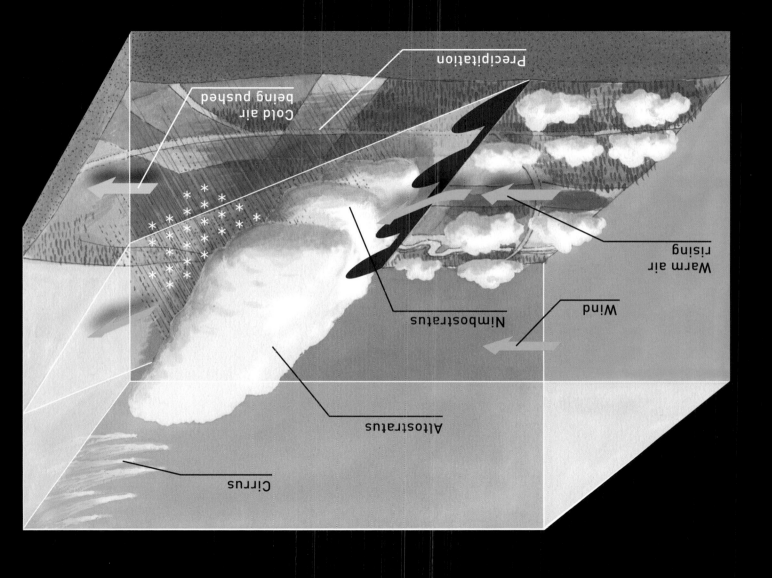

Warm Front

What comes first: thunder or lightning?

A thunderstorm happens every other second somewhere on Earth. They're the most common kind of storm. Thunder gives these storms their name. But it's lightning that causes all the noise. Thunder is the sound of exploding air. Superhot lightning heats and blows up the air it travels through. Lightning is hotter than the surface of the sun. The exploding air creates a shock wave of sound that we hear as rumbles or crashes. Lightning happens in big storm clouds. Ice and water zip up and down inside the storm cloud as winds churn and swirl. All this movement builds up electric charges in the cloud. Lightning gets rid of this charge, like the shock from a doorknob in a carpeted room.

The sound wave of thunder is created at the same time that lightning strikes. But we see the lightning flash first because light travels faster than sound. This is why counting between flashes and rumbles gives you an idea of how far away the lightning struck. The longer the count, the farther the sound had to travel to reach your ears. Thunderstorms bring more than noise and light flashes. They also dump drenching rain, heavy hailstones, and whipping winds, and can even spin out tornadoes.

What makes a tornado twist?

Tornadoes are violent storms with the fastest winds on Earth. The air inside a tornado twirls at speeds up to 300 miles (483 km) per hour! Winds that fierce and fast can do a lot of damage, turning pencils into darts and chunks of wood into missiles. Tornadoes can plow through towns, flattening houses and flipping cars. Fortunately, most tornadoes don't last very long or go very far. A tornado is a very local storm. It can tear up a barn while leaving a nearby shed untouched. Tornadoes are also very sudden storms. One can drop out of a dark sky in an instant.

Tornadoes come from thunderstorms. Most thunderstorms don't make tornadoes, or they can only spin out small ones. Large, forceful, dangerous tornadoes are born in gigantic thunderstorms, called supercells. These huge storms reach high up into the atmosphere, and they are miles wide. The winds inside supercell thunderstorms have the right mix of spinning, pushing, and lifting air to whip up tornadoes. Every spring, giant supercell storms show up in the skies over the Great Plains states. Texas, Oklahoma, Kansas, Nebraska, and Iowa make a line of stacked states pestered by powerful tornadoes. This region is called Tornado Alley. North America isn't the only place plagued by tornadoes. Australia, New Zealand, northern Europe, and western Asia see their share, too.

What are Earth's biggest storms?

Hurricanes are so huge that astronauts can see them from space. The planet's largest storms stretch hundreds of miles across. From a spaceship, a hurricane looks like a disk of swirling thick white clouds with a blue hole in the center. The blue at the bottom of the hole is the ocean. Warm seawater near the equator creates these storms. The air above the sun-soaked seas evaporates water, making warm, humid, rising air that forms clouds. Heat in the air evaporates more water, sending it up into a growing storm. Once the ocean storm has swirling winds of at least 74 miles (119 km) per hour, scientists call it a tropical cyclone.

In the Americas, tropical cyclones are called hurricanes. They are called typhoons in East Asia, and cyclones in the Indian Ocean and Australia. No matter what you call them, these storms last longer, are bigger, and cause more death and destruction than any other. A tropical cyclone can travel for weeks, making a mess over thousands of miles before dying out. A hurricane's strong winds are destructive. But it's the flooding rains and surging seas that more often destroy seaside towns and end lives.

Wind direction

Rainbands

Eyewall

Sinking cool air

Rising warm air

Eye

What's a nor'easter?

A ferocious kind of storm stalks the New England coast in winter. Its strong winds blow in from the ocean in a northeasterly direction. It's why these coastal storms are called nor'easters. Nor'easters bring it all. They dump everything from sleet and snow to flooding rain. The storm's high winds tear up roofs, and giant crashing waves wash away beaches.

Cold temperatures and slick roads make all winter storms dangerous. They often deliver a nasty mix of liquid and frozen precipitation that's hard to predict. Why? A change of only a few degrees in temperature can turn rain to snow, or freezing rain to sleet. A drop of precipitation falling from a cloud travels a long way before hitting the sidewalk. The air it falls through can freeze, melt, and refreeze the precipitation more than once before it lands.

Another kind of winter storm is a blizzard. For scientists to declare a blizzard, the storm must have winds faster than 35 miles (56 km) per hour and falling snow. The blowing wind and snow must also be bad enough to make it hard to see for the next few hours. During a blizzard, travelers can't see more than one-quarter mile (0.4 km) in front of them. That's why driving becomes so dangerous.

Can it snow in a warm climate?

What's the climate where you live? Is it a hot desert, like Arizona? Or is it sub-arctic, like Alaska? A glance out the window won't tell you. What's going on outside your door right now is weather, not climate. The words describe two different things about a place.

Weather is what's going on right now. Climate is what it's usually like outside. You buy clothes to fit your climate. But the weather decides what you'll wear today.

The elements that go into climate are long lasting. They don't change day to day. Arctic climates are colder than tropical climates, because they are farther from the equator and get less sunlight. Mountain climates are shaped by their height, and coastal climates are affected by the ocean. The way global winds circulate around Earth matters, too. Constant, dry winds keep rain from falling in the Sahara desert, for example.

A place's average temperatures and rainfall over a long time decide its climate. One day's weather doesn't make a difference to climate. So while the climate in Hawaii is tropical, today its weather might be cool and rainy. It might even snow.

SNOWY WEATHER EVEN HAPPENS IN DESERT CLIMATES ONCE IN A WHILE.

Is Earth getting warmer?

Weather always changes, while climate is supposed to stay the same. But Earth's climate is currently shifting. The overall temperature of our planet is getting warmer. 2000–2009 was the warmest decade ever recorded. The warm-up started when humans began burning a lot of coal, oil, and gas. These fossil fuels create electricity, power cars, heat homes, and run factories. Unfortunately, they also put carbon dioxide into the air. Carbon dioxide is an invisible gas. It traps heat in the atmosphere, which warms up Earth. Scientists measure and track the amount of carbon dioxide in the atmosphere. As it has increased over the past hundred years, so has the planet's temperature.

A warmer world is causing global climate change. What kinds of changes? Some areas are becoming warmer, but it's not that simple. The global winds and ocean currents that go into climate are changing, too. More extreme storms and flooding will hit some places, while other areas will have less precipitation than normal—drought. Earth is mostly covered in ocean. Melting glaciers and sea ice are raising the level of the sea. This will change coastlines and could sink islands.

We can help reduce the effects of global climate change. Using less energy lowers the amount of carbon dioxide going into the air. Simple things like turning off lights, carpooling, and recycling can help.

ANIMALS THAT LIVE NEAR THE POLES ARE LOSING HOMES BECAUSE OF MELTING SEA ICE.

Can weather scientists predict the future?

If you ever watch the weather forecast, you know they try! Studying and predicting the weather is the job of meteorologists. Thousands of weather stations around the world constantly measure winds, temperature, air pressure, humidity, and rainfall. Satellites, airplanes, radars, ships, and weather balloons also gather information about our atmosphere. Meteorologists use computers to help them collect and study all this weather information. They use it to predict, or forecast, what the weather will be in the future.

A scientist who studies climate is a climatologist. Like weather and climate, the difference between a meteorologist and a climatologist is time. Meteorologists are interested in what's happening now and soon. Climatologists study average rainfall and temperature patterns over decades and centuries. Some climatologists study the past, finding out what the climate was like thousands of years ago. Others are trying to predict Earth's future climate. If you want to study the last Ice Age, become a climatologist. But if you want to track tornadoes, become a meteorologist.

STORM-CHASING METEOROLOGISTS NEED TO TRAVEL IN ARMORED VEHICLES TO COLLECT INFORMATION.

FIND OUT MORE

Books to Read

Breen, Mark and Kathleen Friestad. *The Kids' Book Of Weather Forecasting: Build A Weather Station, "Read" The Sky, & Make Predictions*. Nashville: Ideals Publications, 2003.

Carson, Mary Kay. *Inside Weather*. New York: Sterling, 2011.

Cosgrove, Brian. *Eyewitness: Weather*. London: DK Children, 2007.

Furgang, Kathy. *Everything Weather: Facts, Photos, and Fun that Will Blow Your Mind!*. Washington, D.C.: National Geographic, 2012.

Reilly, Kathleen M. *Explore Weather and Climate!: 25 Great Projects, Activities, Experiments*. White River Junction: Nomad Press, 2011.

Taylor-Butler, Christine. *Meteorology: The Study of Weather*. New York: Children's Press, 2012.

Websites to Visit

A STUDENT'S GUIDE TO GLOBAL CLIMATE CHANGE:
http://www.epa.gov/climatechange/kids

METEOROLOGIST DAN'S WILD WEATHER PAGE:
http://www.wildwildweather.com

NATIONAL WEATHER SERVICE KIDS' PAGE:
http://www.nws.noaa.gov/om/reachout/kidspage.shtml

WEB WEATHER FOR KIDS:
http://eo.ucar.edu/webweather

For bibliography and free activities visit: http://www.sterlingpublishing.com/kids/good-question

INDEX